Learn to Do Yo-Yo Crochet™

General Information

Many of the products used in this pattern book can be purchased from local craft, fabric and variety stores, or from the Annie's Attic Needlecraft Catalog (see Customer Service information on page 32).

Contents

2 Introduction

10 Pumpkin & Spice Hat & Shawl

15 Field of Daisies

18 Harvest Hot Mat

20 Carnival Scarf

22 Snow Amongst the Roses

28 Clover Patch

31 Stitch Guide

32 Metric Conversion Charts

Introduction

Some useful information before beginning will help you understand the basics of the technique so you can design your own patterns.

1. Each yo-yo has the equivalent of 16 double crochet around it. It has 2 sets of chains that are counted as double crochet.

2. Each yo-yo requires 6 chains for its foundation. This helps if you want to make a bigger set of rows than is in this pattern set.

3. All joins are made on 4th and 8th double crochet in a block.

You can do the block with however many yo-yos you want in the center, meaning 1 and 4 for a small square or 1 for hexagon shape and all other numbers (2, 3, 5) will give you

a rectangle; even 4 will if you do a straight line for a row instead of joining them into a square. Just remember each yo-yo has to have 6 chains in the foundation. I also recommend finishing your threads as you go; it's much easier and faster in the long run.

The other bonus to finishing threads as you go is if you make an afghan, you can use it as it grows from lap size to bed size even before you finish the entire afghan.

Special stitches used will be listed with each pattern.

BASIC INSTRUCTIONS

PATTERN NOTE
When joining, drop loop from hook, insert hook in place indicated and pull dropped loop through.

SPECIAL STITCHES
Small shell (sm shell): 3 dc in place indicated.

Small joining shell (sm joining shell): 4 dc in place indicated.

Medium shell (med shell): 7 dc in place indicated.

Large shell (lg shell): 11 dc in place indicated.

Medium joining shell (med joining shell): 8 dc in place indicated.

INSTRUCTIONS
ROW

Row 1: With green, ch 36, **med shell** *(see Special Stitches)* in 3rd ch from hook, *sk next 2 chs**, sc in next ch *(see Photo 1)*, sk next 2 chs, med shell in next ch, rep from * across, ending last rep at **, sl st in next ch *(see Photo 2)*, **do not turn**.

Row 2: Working back across ch on row 1, *med shell in ch at bottom of next med shell**, sc in sp between shells *(see Photo 3)*, rep from * across, ending last rep at **, **join** *(see Pattern Note)*, in 2nd ch of beg ch on row 1. Fasten off *(see Photo 4)*.

Row 3: With ivory, ch 36, **sm joining shell** *(see Special Stitches)* in 3rd ch from hook, join in 4th dc of first yo-yo, **sm shell** *(see Special Stitches)* in same ch as last sm joining shell, *sk next 2 chs**, sc in next ch *(see Photo 5)*, sk next 2 chs, (sm joining shell, join in 4th dc of next yo-yo, sm shell) in next ch, rep from * across, ending last rep at **, sl st in last ch, **do not turn**.

Row 4: Working back across ch of last row, med shell in ch at bottom of next shell, [sc in sp between shells *(see Photo 6)*, med shell in ch at bottom of next med shell] across, join in 2nd ch of beg ch of last row *(see Photo 7)*. Fasten off.

8

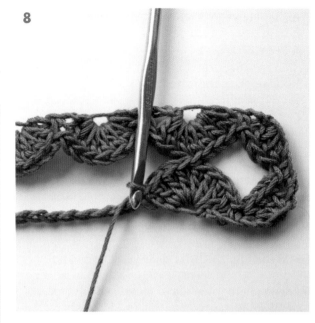

6

7

9

DOUBLE ROW

Rnd 5: Now working in rnds, with rust, ch 72, sm shell in 3rd ch from hook, [sk next 2 chs, sc in next ch, sk next 2 chs, med shell in next ch] 4 times, [sk next 2 chs, sc in next ch, sk next 2 chs, sm shell in next ch] twice, [sk next 2 chs, sc in next ch, sk next 2 chs, (sm joining shell, join to 4th dc of last med shell worked, sm shell) in next ch *(see Photo 8)*] 4 times, sk next 2 chs, sc in next ch, sk next 2 chs, sm joining shell in next ch, join to 2nd ch of beg ch-2, sk next 2 sts, sl st in last ch *(see Photo 9)*.

Rnd 6: Working on opposite side of ch of rnd 5, **med joining shell** *(see Special Stitches)* in ch at bottom of last sm shell worked, join to center dc of first yo-yo on last row, sm shell in same ch, [sc in sp between shells *(see Photo 10)*, (sm joining shell, join to center dc of next yo-yo, sm shell) in ch at bottom of next shell] 4 times, sc in sp between shells, (sm joining shell, join to center dc of next yo-yo, med shell) in ch at bottom of next shell, sc in sp between shells, **lg shell** *(see Special Stitches)* in ch at bottom of next shell, sc in sp between next shells *(see Photo 11)*, [med shell in ch at bottom of next shell, sc in sp between shell] 4 times, lg shell in ch of next sm shell, sc in sp between yo-yos, join in beg dc of first med joining shell (see Photo 12). Fasten off.

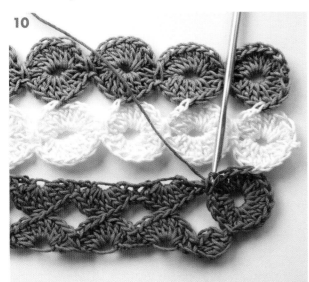

10

11

12

BLOCK
CENTER SQUARE

Rnd 1: Ch 24, **sm shell** (see Special Stitches) in 3rd ch from hook (first 2 chs count as first dc), [sk next 2 chs (see Photo 1), sc in next ch, sk next 2 chs, sm shell in next ch] across (see Photo 2), sk next 2 chs, sc in last ch, **join** (see Pattern Note) in 2nd ch of beg ch-2 (see Photos 3 & 4). **Do not turn.**

1

2

3

4

Rnd 2: [**Lg shell** (*see Special Stitches*) in same ch as sm shell is worked, working over sc on last rnd, sc in sp between sm shells (*see Photo 5*)] around, join in beg dc (*see Photo 6*). Fasten off.

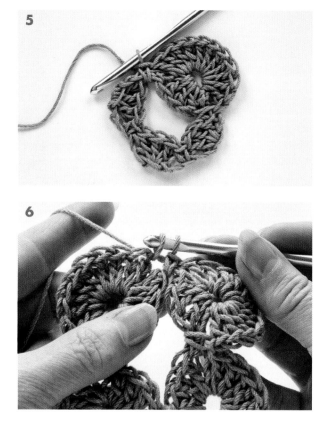

Place marker in 4th dc of any lg shell (*see Photo 7*).

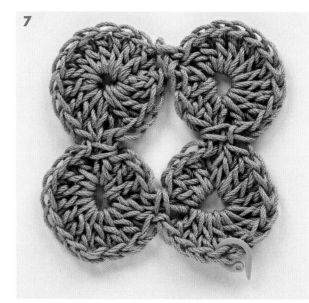

OUTER SQUARE

Rnd 1: Ch 72, sm shell in 3rd ch from hook (*corner*), sk next 2 chs, sc in next ch, work the following steps to complete this rnd:

A. Sk next 2 chs, **sm joining shell** (*see Special Stitches*) in next ch, join in marked st on Center Square Large Shell, move marker to 4th dc of next large shell (*see Photo 8*), sm shell in same ch as sm joining shell, sk next 2 chs, sc in next ch;

B. Sk next 2 chs, sm joining shell in next ch, join in next marked st, move marker to 8th st of this same shell, sm shell in same ch as sm joining shell, sk next 2 chs, sc in next ch;

C. Sk next 2 chs, sm shell in next ch (*corner*), sk next 2 chs, sc in next ch (*see Photo 9*), sk next 2 chs, sm joining shell in next ch, join to marked dc, move marker to 4th dc of next lg shell, sk next 2 chs, sc in next ch;

D. [Rep steps B and C] twice;

E. Sk next 2 chs, sm joining shell in next ch, join in next marked st, sm shell in same ch as sm joining shell, sk next 2 chs, sc in last ch, join in 2nd ch of beg ch-2 *(see Photo 10).*

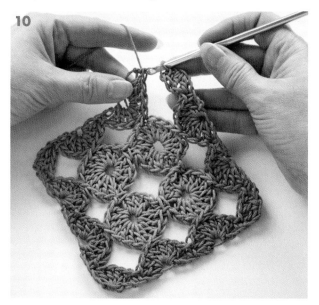

Rnd 2: *[**Med shell** *(see Special Stitches)* in bottom of same ch as sm joining shell and sm shell *(see Photo 11)*, sc in sp between shells as shown in photo 11] twice, lg shell in bottom of same ch on corner sm shell, sc in next sp between shells *(see Photo 12)*, rep from * around, join in top of beg dc on first med shell *(see Photo 13)*. Fasten off.

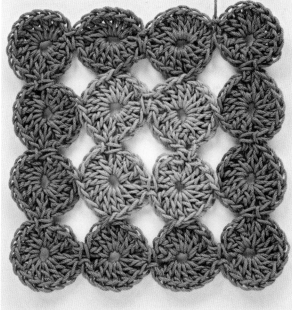

Block is now completed.

JOINING TO OTHER BLOCKS

When you have finished your Block and want to add it to another, this is done during the last round of the Block.

First, you will have to make your chain the correct length for the round according to chain number list, and then do the first half of round joining to previous round; start 2nd half of round. This is after you have gone all the way around the Block once and joined to the beginning chain. When you get to the first complete corner of the 2nd corner of the 2nd half of the round, start your joins.

JOINING BLOCK
CENTER SQUARE

Work same as Center Square on First Block.

OUTER SQUARE

Rnd 1: Work same as rnd 1 of Outer Square on First Block.

Rnd 2: *[Med shell in bottom of same ch as sm joining shell and sm shell, sc in sp between shells] twice**, lg shell in bottom of same ch on corner sm shell, sc in next sp between shells, rep from * twice, ending last rep at **, **med joining shell** *(see Special Stitches)* in next corner sm shell, join to 8th dc on corresponding corner of last Block *(see Photo 14)*, sm shell in same corner sm shell, [sc in sp between shells, sm joining shell in bottom ch of next sm joining shell and sm shell, join in 4th dc on corresponding shell of last Block, sm shell in same ch as last sm joining shell] twice, sc in sp between shells, sm joining shell in bottom of ch on last corner sm shell, join in 4th dc on corresponding corner of last Block, med shell in same ch as last sm joining shell, join in beg dc *(see Photo 15)*. Fasten off.

If you make several of these Squares and join them end to end, you can have a cute scarf for winter, or with a starting chain for the first 14 rows, this can make a nice baby blanket for a car seat.

14

15

CHAIN NUMBER LIST

1. 6 chains x 4 yo-yos = 24 chains per round or row;

2. 6 chains x 12 yo-yos = 72 chains per round or row;

3. 6 chains x 20 yo-yos = 120 chains per round or row;

4. 6 chains x 28 yo-yos = 168 chains per round or row;

5. 6 chains x 36 yo-yos = 216 chains per round or row;

6. 6 chains x 44 yo-yos = 264 chains per round or row;

7. 6 chains x 52 yo-yos = 312 chains per round or row;

8. 6 chains x 60 yo-yos = 360 chains per round or row;

9. 6 chains x 68 yo-yos = 408 chains per round or row;

10. 6 chains x 76 yo-yos = 456 chains per round or row;

11. 6 chains x 81 yo-yos = 486 chains per round or row;

12. 6 chains x 89 yo-yos = 534 chains per round or row;

13. 6 chains x 97 yo-yos = 582 chains per round or row;

14. 6 chains x 105 yo-yos = 630 chains per round or row.

If you want to go beyond this, each round has 48 chains more than the previous round. So add 48 to the next round, and then on and on, or you can take the number of yo-yos per round and just multiply by 6. This will give you the same answer. Each round has 8 more yo-yos than the previous round.

This is a fun technique; you can make, afghans, scarves, headbands, necklaces, bracelets, belts, edgings and more. It is a technique to be applied as your imagination lets you. ∎

Pumpkin & Spice
Hat & Shawl

HAT
SKILL LEVEL

INTERMEDIATE

FINISHED SIZE
One size fits most

MATERIALS
- Omega Alegria light (light worsted) weight yarn (3½ oz/186 yds/100g per skein):
    1 skein each #07 papaya, #25 brown, #85 citrus and #22 beige
- Size E/4/3.5mm crochet hook or size needed to obtain gauge

3 LIGHT

GAUGE
1 yo-yo = 1¼ inches in diameter

PATTERN NOTES
Stitches used in this pattern are found in the Stitch Guide unless otherwise stated in Special Stitches.

Read Information on pages 2–9 before beginning.

Chain-2 at beginning of row or round counts as first double crochet unless otherwise stated.

When joining, drop loop from hook, insert hook in place indicated and pull dropped loop through.

If you would like your Hat a little longer, make 3 rounds of yo-yos instead of 2. The item in the photo with 2 rounds reaches just below the top of the ear on the average person, and with 3 rounds, it reaches just above the bottom of the ear. If you decide to make the extra round of yo-yos, begin with papaya instead of citrus, then citrus and brown.

SPECIAL STITCHES
Small shell (sm shell): 3 dc in place indicated.

Small joining shell (sm joining shell): 4 dc in place indicated.

Medium shell (med shell): 7 dc in place indicated.

INSTRUCTIONS
HAT
TOP
Rnd 1: With papaya, ch 6, sl st in first ch to form ring, **ch 2** (see Pattern Notes), 11 dc in ring, **join** (see Pattern Notes) in 2nd ch of beg ch-2. (12 dc)

Rnd 2: Ch 2, dc in same st, 2 dc in each st around, join in 2nd ch of beg ch-2. *(24 dc)*

Rnd 3: Ch 2, dc in same st, dc in next st, [2 dc in next st, dc in next st] around, join in 2nd ch of beg ch-2. *(36 dc)*

Rnd 4: Ch 2, dc in same st, dc in each of next 2 sts, [2 dc in next st, dc in each of next 2 sts] around, join in 2nd ch of beg ch-2. *(48 dc)*

Rnd 5: Ch 2, dc in same st, dc in each of next 3 sts, [2 dc in next st, dc in each of next 3 sts] around, join in 2nd ch of beg ch-2. *(60 dc)*

Rnd 6: Ch 2, dc in same st, dc in each of next 4 sts, [2 dc in next st, dc in each of next 4 sts] around, join in 2nd ch of beg ch-2. *(72 dc)*

Rnd 7: Ch 2, dc in same st, dc in each of next 5 sts, [2 dc in next st, dc in each of next 5 sts] around, join in 2nd ch of beg ch-2. *(84 dc)*

Rnd 8: Ch 2, dc in same st, dc in each of next 6 sts, [2 dc in next st, dc in each of next 6 sts] around, join in 2nd ch of beg ch-2. *(96 dc)*

SIDES

Rnd 1: With citrus, ch 96, **sm joining shell** *(see Special Stitches)* in 3rd ch from hook, join to any dc on last rnd of Top, **sm shell** *(see Special Stitches)* in same ch as sm joining shell, *sk next 2 chs, sc in next ch, sk next 2 chs**, sm joining shell in next ch, sk next 5 dc on Top, join in next dc, sm shell in same ch, rep from * around Top of Hat, ending last rep at **, sl st in last ch, join in 2nd ch of beg ch-2.

Rnd 2: [**Med shell** *(see Special Stitches)* in bottom of same ch as first sm joining shell, sc in sp between shells] around, join in beg dc of first med shell. Fasten off.

Rnd 3: With brown, ch 96, sm joining shell in 3rd ch from hook, join to center dc on any yo-yo on rnd 2, sm shell in same ch, *sk next 2 chs, sc in next ch, sk next 2 chs**, small joining shell in next ch, join to center dc of next yo-yo, sm shell in same ch, rep from * around, ending last rep at **, sl st in last ch, join in 2nd ch of beg ch-2.

Rnd 4: Rep rnd 2.

EDGING

Rnd 1: With beige, join with sc to center dc of any yo-yo, ch 3, *dc in sc between yo-yos, ch 3**, sc in center dc of next yo-yo, ch 3, rep from * around, ending last rep at **, join in beg sc.

Rnd 2: Ch 2, 6 dc in same st, *sc in next dc**, 7 dc in next sc, rep from * around, ending last rep at **, join in 2nd ch of beg ch-2. Fasten off.

SHAWL
SKILL LEVEL

INTERMEDIATE

FINISHED SIZE
One size fits most

MATERIALS
- Omega Alegria light (light worsted) weight yarn (3½ oz/186yds/100g per ball):
    3 balls each #07 papaya, #25 brown, #85 citrus and #22 beige
- Size E/4/3.5mm crochet hook or size needed to obtain gauge
- Stitch marker

GAUGE
1 yo-yo = 1¼ inches in diameter

PATTERN NOTES
Stitches used in this pattern are found in the Stitch Guide unless otherwise stated in Special Stitches.

Read Information on pages 2–9 before beginning.

Chain-2 at beginning of row or round counts as first double crochet unless otherwise stated.

When joining, drop loop from hook, insert hook in place indicated and pull dropped loop through.

If you would like a longer Shawl, each row has 24 chains more than the previous row. You may add as many rows as desired.

SPECIAL STITCHES
Small shell (sm shell): 3 dc in place indicated.

Small joining shell (sm joining shell): 4 dc in place indicated.

Medium shell (med shell): 7 dc in place indicated.

Large shell (lg shell): 11 dc in place indicated.

INSTRUCTIONS
SHAWL
Row 1: With papaya, ch 3, 15 dc in 3rd ch from hook (*first 2 chs count as first dc*), **join** (*see Pattern Notes*) in 2nd ch of beg ch-2 (*yo-yo completed*). (*16 dc*)

Row 2: With beige, ch 30, **med shell** (*see Special Stitches*) in 3rd ch from hook, sk next 2 chs, sc in next ch, sk next 2 chs, **sm joining shell** (*see Special Stitches*) in next ch, join to any dc of row 1, **sm shell** (*see Special Stitches*) in same ch as last sm joining shell, sk next 2 chs, sc in next ch, sk next 2 chs, sm shell in next ch (*corner*), sk next 2 chs, sc in next ch, sk next 2 chs, sm joining shell in next ch, sk next 3 dc on row 1, join in next dc, sm shell in same ch as last sm joining shell, sk next 2 chs, sc in next ch, sk next 2 chs, med shell in next ch, sk next 2 chs, sl st in last ch.

Row 3: Working in bottom of ch on last row, [med shell in bottom of same ch of med shell, sc in sp between shells] twice, **lg shell** (*see Special Stitches*) in ch at bottom of corner shell, sc in sp between shells, med shell in ch at bottom of next shell, sc in next sp between shells, med shell in ch at bottom of first med shell, join in 2nd ch of beg ch-2. Fasten off.

Row 4: With citrus, ch 54, med shell in 3rd ch from hook, sk next 2 chs, sc in next ch, sk next 2 chs, work the following steps to complete the row:

A. (Sm joining shell, join to center dc of first yo-yo on last row, sm shell) in next ch;

B. Sk next 2 chs, sc in next ch, sk next 2 chs;

C. [Joining in next yo-yo, rep steps A and B] twice;

D. Sm shell in next ch (corner), joining in next yo-yo, rep step B;

E. [Joining in next yo-yo, rep steps A and B] twice;

F. Med shell in next ch, sk next 2 chs, sl st in last ch.

Row 5: Working back across ch of row 4, med shell in same ch as last med shell, [sc between shells, med shell in same ch as next shell] twice, sc in sp between shells, lg shell in same ch as corner, [sc in sp between shells, med shell in same ch as next shell] across, join in 2nd ch of beg ch-2 on last row. Fasten off.

Row 6: With brown, ch 78, med shell in 3rd ch from hook, sk next 2 chs, sc in next ch, sk next 2 chs, work the following steps to complete the row:

A. (Sm joining shell, join to center dc of first yo-yo on last row, sm shell) in next ch;

B. Sk next 2 chs, sc in next ch, sk next 2 chs;

C. [Joining in next yo-yo, rep steps A and B] as needed to reach corner;

D. Sm shell in next ch (corner), rep step B;

E. [Joining in next yo-yo, rep steps A and B] across to last 4 chs;

F. Med shell in next ch, sk next 2 chs, sl st in last ch.

Row 7: Working back across ch of row 6, med shell in same ch as last med shell, [sc in sp between shells, med shell in same ch as next shell] as needed to reach corner, sc in sp between shells, lg shell in same ch as corner, [sc in sp between shells, med shell in same ch as next shell] across, join in 2nd ch of beg ch-2 on last row. Fasten off.

Next rows: Rep rows 6 and 7 consecutively until you have 20 rows or desired length of completed yo-yos, adding 24 chs each time to row 6 and working in color sequence of beige, citrus, brown and papaya, or as desired.

Mark joining of last row.

EDGING
Rnd 1: With RS facing and working across top edge in end yo-yos only, join beige with sc in marked st on last row of Shawl, [ch 3, sk next 3 dc, sc in next dc on same yo-yo, ch 5, hdc in 3rd dc from joining on next yo-yo] across ending in last yo-yo at opposite end of top edge, [ch 3, sk next 3 dc, sc in next dc on same yo-yo] twice, [ch 3, dc in sc between shells, ch 3, sk next 3 dc on next yo-yo, sc in next dc] across to corner yo-yo, ch 3, sk next 3 dc on last yo-yo, sc in next dc on same corner yo-yo, [ch 3, dc in sc between shells, ch 3, sk next 3 dc on next yo-yo, sc in next dc] across, ending last sc on same yo-yo as first sc of last row, ch 3, sk next 3 dc on first yo-yo, join in beg sc.

Rnd 2: Ch 2, 6 dc in same st, sc in next ch sp, [med shell in next st, sc in next ch sp] across to opposite end of top edge, [med shell in next st, sc in next dc] across to corner, med shell in next st, sc in next ch sp, [med shell in next st, sc in next dc] across, med shell in next st, sc in last ch sp, join in 2nd ch of beg ch-2. Fasten off. ■

Field of
Daisies

SKILL LEVEL
INTERMEDIATE

FINISHED SIZE
40 x 42 inches

MATERIALS
- Plymouth Yarn Co. Jeannee Worsted medium (worsted) weight yarn (1¾ oz/110 yds/50g per ball):
  6 balls #17 yellow
  5 balls each #14 white and #100 variegated
- Size H/8/5mm crochet hook or size needed to obtain gauge

GAUGE
1 yo-yo = 1¼ inches in diameter

PATTERN NOTES
Stitches used in this pattern are found in the Stitch Guide unless otherwise stated in Special Stitches.

When joining, drop loop from hook, insert hook in place indicated and pull dropped loop through.

SPECIAL STITCHES
Small shell (sm shell): 3 dc in place indicated.

Small joining shell (sm joining shell): 4 dc in place indicated.

Medium shell (med shell): 7 dc in place indicated.

Large shell (lg shell): 11 dc in place indicated.

INSTRUCTIONS
BLANKET
CENTER
CENTER SQUARE
MAKE 10.
Rnd 1: With yellow, ch 24, **sm shell** (*see Special Stitches*) in 3rd ch from hook (*first 2 chs count as first dc*), [sk next 2 chs (*see Photo 1 on page 5*), sc in next ch, sk next 2 chs, sm shell in next ch] across (*see Photo 2*), sk next 2 chs, sl st in last ch, **join** (*see Pattern Notes*) in 2nd ch of beg ch-2 (*see Photos 3 and 4 on page 5*). **Do not turn.**

Rnd 2: [**Lg shell** (*see Special Stitches*) in same ch as sm shell is worked, sc in sp between sm shells (*see Photo 5 on page 6*)] around, join in beg dc (*see Photo 6 on page 6*). Fasten off.

ZIGZAG
FIRST SIDE
Row 1: With variegated, ch 246, **sm joining shell** (*see Special Stitches*) in 3rd ch from hook, join to dc 4 sts to right of any sc on 1 Square, sm shell in same ch as sm joining shell, work the following steps to complete row:

A. Sk next 2 chs, sc in next ch, sk next 2 chs;

B. Sm joining shell in next ch, join to 4th dc on next yo-yo on same Square, sm shell in same ch as sm joining shell;

C. Rep step A;

D. Sm shell in next ch *(corner)*;

E. Rep step A;

F. Sm joining shell in next ch, sk next 3 sts on same yo-yo as last worked in, join in next st, sm shell in same ch as sm joining shell;

G. Rep step A;

H. Sm joining shell in next ch, join to 4th dc on next yo-yo on same Square, sm joining shell in same ch, join to 4th dc on the next yo-yo on next Square, sm shell in same ch as 2 sm joining shells;

I. [Rep steps A–H consecutively] 9 times, ending last rep with step F;

J. Rep steps A and B, sk next 2 chs, sl st in last ch, **do not turn.**

Row 2: Working back across row 1, **med shell** *(see Special Stitches)* in ch at bottom of last shell, *sc in sp between shells, med shell in ch at bottom of next shell, sc in sp between shells, lg shell in ch at bottom of next shell at corner, [sc in sp between shells, med shell in next ch at bottom of next shell] twice, rep from * across, join in 2nd ch of beg ch-2 of last row. Fasten off.

Row 3: With yellow, ch 246, sm joining shell in 3rd ch from hook, sk first yo-yo on last row, join in 4th dc on 2nd yo-yo, sm shell in same ch as last sm joining shell, work the following steps to complete row:

A. Sk next 2 chs, sc in next ch, sk next 2 chs;

B. Sm joining shell in next ch, join to 4th dc on next yo-yo, sm shell in same ch as sm joining shell;

C. Rep step A;

D. Sm shell in next ch *(corner)*;

E. Rep step A;

F. Sm joining shell in next ch, sk next 3 sts on same yo-yo as last worked in, join in next st, sm shell in same ch as sm joining shell;

G. Rep step A;

H. Sm joining shell in next ch, join to 4th dc on next yo-yo, sm joining shell in same ch, sk next yo-yo at center, join to 4th dc of next yo-yo, sm shell in same ch as 2 sm joining shells;

I. [Rep steps A–H consecutively] 9 times, ending last rep with step F;

J. Rep steps A and B, sk next 2 chs, sl st in last ch, **do not turn.**

Row 4: Working back across row 1, med shell in ch at bottom of last shell, *sc in sp between shells, med shell in ch at bottom of next shell, sc in sp between shells, lg shell in ch at bottom of next shell at corner, [sc in sp between shells, med shell in next ch at bottom of next shell] twice, rep from * across, join in 2nd ch of beg ch-2 of last row. Fasten off.

Rows 5 & 6: With white, rep rows 3 and 4.

Rows 7 & 8: Rep rows 3 and 4.

Rows 9 & 10: With white, rep rows 3 and 4.

Rows 11 & 12: With variegated, rep rows 3 and 4.

Rows 13 & 14: With white, rep rows 3 and 4.

Rows 15 & 16: With variegated, rep rows 3 and 4.

Rows 17 & 18: Rep rows 3 and 4.

2ND SIDE
Working on rem side of Squares, rep First Side. ∎

Harvest Hot Mat

SKILL LEVEL

◼◼◼◻
INTERMEDIATE

FINISHED SIZE
10½ inches square

MATERIALS
- Pisgah Yarn and Dyeing Co. Peaches & Creme medium (worsted) weight cotton yarn (2 oz/98 yds/57g per ball):
  1 ball #180 peppercorn ombre
- Size I/9/5.5mm crochet hook or size needed to obtain gauge

GAUGE
1 yo-yo = 1¾ inches in diameter

PATTERN NOTES
Stitches used in this pattern are found in the Stitch Guide unless otherwise stated in Special Stitches.

When joining, drop loop from hook, insert hook in place indicated and pull dropped loop through.

SPECIAL STITCHES
Small shell (sm shell): 3 dc in place indicated.

Small joining shell (sm joining shell): 4 dc in place indicated.

Medium shell (med shell): 7 dc in place indicated.

Large shell (lg shell): 11 dc in place indicated.

INSTRUCTIONS
HOT MAT
CENTER SQUARE
Rnd 1: Ch 24, **sm shell** (*see Special Stitches*) in 3rd ch from hook (*first 2 chs count as first dc*), sk next 2 chs (*see Photo 1 on page 5*), sc in next ch, [sk next 2 chs, sm shell in next ch, sk next 2 chs, sc in next ch] across (*see Photo 2*), **join** (*see Pattern Notes*) in 2nd ch of beg ch-2 (*see Photos 3 and 4 on page 5*). **Do not turn.**

Rnd 2: [**Lg shell** (*see Special Stitches*) in same ch as sm shell is worked, sc in sp between sm shells (*see Photo 5 on page 6*)] around, join in beg dc (*see Photo 6 on page 6*). Fasten off.

Place marker in 4th dc of any lg shell (*see Photo 7 on page 6*).

NEXT SQUARE
Rnd 1: Ch 72, small shell in 3rd ch from hook (*corner*), sk next 2 chs, sc in next ch, work the following steps to complete this rnd:

A. Sk next 2 chs, **sm joining shell** (*see Special Stitches*) in next ch, join in marked st on Center Square Lg Shell, move marker to 4th dc of next large shell (*see Photo 8 on page 6*), sm shell in same ch as sm joining shell, sk next 2 chs, sc in next ch;

B. Sk next 2 chs, sm joining shell in next ch, join in next marked st, move marker to 8th st of this same shell, sm shell in same ch as sm joining shell, sk next 2 chs, sc in next ch;

C. Sk next 2 chs, sm shell in next ch (*corner*), sk next 2 chs, sc in next ch (*see Photo 9 on page 6*), sk next 2 chs, sm joining shell in next ch, join to marked dc, move marker to 4th dc of next lg shell, sm shell in same ch as sm joining shell, sc in next ch, sk next 2 chs;

D. [Rep steps B and C] twice;

E. Sk next 2 chs, sm joining shell in next ch, join in next marked st, sm shell in same ch as sm joining shell, sk next 2 chs, sc in next ch, join in 2nd ch of beg ch-2 *(see Photo 10 on page 7)*.

Rnd 2: *[**Med shell** *(see Special Stitches)* in bottom of same ch as sm joining shell and sm shell *(see Photo 11 on page 7)*, sc in sp between shells as shown in photo 11] twice, lg shell in bottom of same ch on corner sm shell, sc in next sp between shells *(see Photo 12 on page 7)*, rep from * around, join in top of beg dc on first med shell *(see Photo 13 on page 7)*. Fasten off.

Place marker in 4th dc of any lg shell of last rnd.

LAST SQUARE
Rnd 1: Ch 120, sm shell in 3rd ch from hook, small shell in 3rd ch from hook *(corner)*, sk next 2 chs, sc in next ch, work the following steps to complete this rnd:

A. [Sk next 2 chs, sm joining shell in next ch, join in marked st on Center Square Large

Shell, move marker to 4th dc of next lg shell, sm shell in same ch as sm joining shell, sk next 2 chs, sc in next ch] twice;

B. Sk next 2 chs, sm joining shell in next ch, join in next marked st, move marker to 8th st of this same shell, sm shell in same ch as sm joining shell, sk next 2 chs, sc in next ch;

C. Sk next 2 chs, sm shell in next ch *(corner)*, sk next 2 chs, sc in next ch, [sk next 2 chs, sm joining shell in next ch, join to marked dc, move marker to 4th dc of next med shell, sm shell in same ch as sm joining shell, sk next 2 chs, sc in next ch] 3 times;

D. [Rep steps B and C] twice;

E. Sk next 2 chs, sm joining shell in next ch, join in next marked st, sm shell in same ch as sm joining shell, sk next 2 chs, sc in next ch, join in 2nd ch of beg ch-2.

Rnd 2: Rep rnd 2 of Next Square. ∎

Carnival Scarf

SKILL LEVEL

◧◼◼◻
INTERMEDIATE

FINISHED SIZE
5¾ x 47 inches

MATERIALS
- Pisgah Yarn and Dyeing Co. Honeysuckle Rayon Chenille light (light worsted) weight yarn (88 yds per ball):
  3 balls #128 passion
  2 balls #23 ruby
- Size I/9/5.5mm crochet hook or size needed to obtain gauge

GAUGE
1 yo-yo = 1¼ inches in diameter

PATTERN NOTES
Stitches used in this pattern are found in the Stitch Guide unless otherwise stated in Special Stitches.

When joining, drop loop from hook, insert hook in place indicated and pull dropped loop through.

SPECIAL STITCHES
Small shell (sm shell): 3 dc in place indicated.

Small joining shell (sm joining shell): 4 dc in place indicated.

Medium shell (med shell): 7 dc in place indicated.

INSTRUCTIONS
SCARF
Row 1: With passion, ch 216, **med shell** (see Special Stitches) in 3rd ch from hook, *sk next 2 chs**, sc in next ch, sk next 2 chs, med shell in next ch, rep from * across, ending last rep at **, sl st in last ch, **do not turn.**

Row 2: Working back across ch on row 1, *med shell in ch at bottom of next med shell**, sc in sp between shells, rep from * across, ending last rep at **, **join** (see Pattern Notes) in 2nd ch of beg ch on row 1. Fasten off.

Row 3: With passion, ch 216, **sm joining shell** (see Special Stitches) in 3rd ch from hook, join in 4th dc of first yo-yo, small shell in same ch as last sm joining shell, *sk next 2 chs**, sc in next ch, sk next 2 chs, (sm joining shell, join in 4th dc of next yo-yo, **sm shell**—see Special Stitches) in next ch, rep from * across, ending last rep at **, sl st in last ch, **do not turn.**

Row 4: Working back across ch of last row, med shell in ch at bottom of next shell, [sc in sp between shells, med shell in ch at bottom of next med shell] across, join in 2nd ch of beg ch of last row. Fasten off.

Rows 5 & 6: Rep rows 3 and 4.

EDGING
Rnd 1: Working across 1 short end, join ruby with sc in center dc of first yo-yo, *ch 3, dc in sp between yo-yos, ch 3, sk next 3 dc on next yo-yo, sc in next dc, ch 3, dc in sp between yo-yos, ch 3, sk next 3 sts on next yo-yo, sc in next dc, sk next 3 dc on same yo-yo, sc in next dc, ch 3, [dc in sp between yo-yos, ch 3, sc in center dc of next yo-yo, ch 3] across** ending in last yo-yo, sk next 3 dc of same yo-yo, sc in next dc, rep from * around, ending last rep at **, join in beg sc.

Rnd 2: Ch 2, 6 dc in same st, sc in each dc and 7 dc in each sc around, join in 2nd ch of beg ch-2. Fasten off. ∎

Snow
Amongst the Roses

LAPGHAN
SKILL LEVEL

INTERMEDIATE

FINISHED SIZE
78¾ inches across

MATERIALS
- Red Heart Classic medium (worsted) weight yarn (3½ oz/ 190 yds/99g per skein):
  - 7 skeins #1 white
  - 6 skeins #615 artichoke
  - 4 skeins #759 cameo rose
  - 2 skeins #760 new berry
  - 1 skein #339 mid brown
- Size J/10/6mm crochet hook or size needed to obtain gauge

GAUGE
1 yo-yo = 1¾ inches in diameter

PATTERN NOTES
Stitches used in this pattern are found in the Stitch Guide unless otherwise stated in Special Stitches.

When joining, drop loop from hook, insert hook in place indicated and pull dropped loop through.

SPECIAL STITCHES
Small shell (sm shell): 3 dc in place indicated.

Medium shell (med shell): 9 dc in place indicated.

Large shell (lg shell): 12 dc in place indicated.

Corner A: (7 dc, join in 5th or 7th dc on corresponding yo-yo, 5 dc) in ch at bottom of next sm shell.

Corner B: (5 dc, join in 5th or 7th dc of corresponding yo-yo, 7 dc) in ch at bottom of next sm shell.

Corner C: (5 dc, join to 5th dc of corresponding yo-yo, 2 dc, sk next 2 dc on same corresponding yo-yo, join in next dc, 5 dc) in ch at bottom of next sm shell.

INSTRUCTIONS
LAPGHAN
FIRST MOTIF
Rnd 1: With mid brown, ch 3, 17 dc in 3rd ch from hook (*rem 2 chs of beg ch-3 counts as first dc*), **join** (*see Pattern Notes*) in 3rd ch of beg ch-3. Fasten off.

Rnd 2: With new berry, ch 36, 2 dc in 3rd ch from hook (*first 2 chs count as first dc*), join to any dc on rnd 1, 3 dc in same ch as last dc, *sk next 2 chs, sc in next ch**, sk next 2 chs, 2 dc in next ch, sk next 2 dc on rnd 1, join in next dc, **sm shell** (*see Special Stitches*) in same ch as last dc, rep from * around, ending last rep at **, join in 2nd ch of beg 2 chs. **Do not turn.**

Rnd 3: Lg shell (*see Special Stitches*) in ch at bottom of each sm shell around with sc between shells, join in beg dc of first large shell. Fasten off.

Rnd 4: With cameo rose, ch 72, 2 dc in 3rd ch from hook, join to 6th dc to left of any sc on last rnd, sm shell in same ch as last dc (*corner*), work the following steps to complete rnd:

A. Sk next 2 chs, sc in next ch, sk next 2 chs;

B. 2 dc in next ch, sk next 2 dc on same yo-yo, join in next dc in same yo-yo as last joining, sm shell in same ch as last dc, join in 3rd dc on next yo-yo, 2 dc in same ch as last dc;

C. Rep step A;

D. 2 dc in next ch, sk next 2 dc on same yo-yo of last rnd, join in next dc, sm shell in same ch as last dc;

E. Rep steps A–D around, ending last rep with step B;

F. Sk next 2 chs, sc in last ch, join in 3rd ch of beg ch-3. **Do not turn.**

Rnd 5: Lg shell in same ch at bottom of next sm shell, sc in sp between shells, **med shell** (see Special Stitches) in ch at bottom of each sm shell around with sc between shells and lg shell in each corner, join in first dc of beg large shell. Fasten off.

Rnd 6: With artichoke, ch 108, 2 dc in 3rd ch from hook, join to 6th dc to left of any sc on last rnd at corner, sm shell in same ch as last dc (corner), work the following steps to complete rnd:

A. Sk next 2 chs, sc in next ch, sk next 2 chs;

B. 2 dc in next ch, sk next 2 dc on same yo-yo, join in next dc in same yo-yo as last joining, sm shell in same ch as last dc, join in 3rd dc on next yo-yo, 2 dc in same ch as last dc;

C. Rep steps A, B and A;

D. 2 dc in next ch, sk next 2 dc on same yo-yo of last rnd, join in next dc, sm shell in same ch as last dc (corner);

E. Rep steps A–D around, ending last rep with step B;

F. Sk next 2 chs, sc in last ch, join in 3rd ch of beg ch-3. **Do not turn.**

Rnd 7: Lg shell in same ch at bottom of next sm shell, sc in sp between shells, med shell in ch at bottom of each sm shell around with sc in sp between shells and lg shell in each corner, join in first dc of beg large shell. Fasten off.

Rnd 8: With white, ch 144, 2 dc in 3rd ch from hook, join to 6th dc to left of any sc on last rnd at corner, sm shell in same ch as last dc (corner), work the following steps to complete rnd:

A. Sk next 2 chs, sc in next ch, sk next 2 chs;

B. 2 dc in next ch, sk next 2 dc on same yo-yo, join in next dc in same yo-yo as last joining, sm shell in same ch as last dc, join in 3rd dc on next yo-yo, 2 dc in same ch as last dc (corner);

C. [Rep steps A and B] twice, rep step A;

D. 2 dc in next ch, sk next 2 dc on same yo-yo of last rnd, join in next dc, sm shell in same ch as last dc (corner);

E. Rep steps A–D around;

F. Sk next ch, sc in last ch, join in 3rd ch of beg ch-3. **Do not turn.**

Rnd 9: Lg shell in same ch at bottom of next sm shell at corner, sc in sp between shells, med shell in ch at bottom of each sm shell around with sc between shells and lg shell in each corner, join in first dc of beg large shell. Fasten off.

1-SIDE JOINED MOTIF
Rnds 1–8: Rep rnds 1–8 of First Motif.

Rnd 9: Lg shell in ch at bottom on next sm shell, sc in sp between shells, [med shell in ch at bottom of next small shell, sc in sp between next shells] 3 times, work the following steps to complete this rnd;

A. **Corner A** (see Special Stitches) according to photo placement;

B. Sc in sp between yo-yos;

C. 4 dc in ch at bottom of next sm shell, join to 5th dc in next yo-yo on last Motif, 4 dc in same ch as last dc, rep step B;

D. Rep step C across to next corner;

E. **Corner B** (see Special Stitches), rep step B (steps A–E complete joining);

F. Med shell in ch at bottom of each sm shell around with sc between shells and lg shell in each corner, join in beg dc. Fasten off.

ASSEMBLY

Work 4 1-Side Joined Motifs, joining to bottom of Motifs as shown in photo across center, joining on 2 or more sides using **Corners A, B and C** *(see Special Stitches)* according to photo.

Work a row of 4 Motifs on each side of center row as shown in photo.

Work a row of 3 Motifs on each side of last row of Motifs as shown in photo.

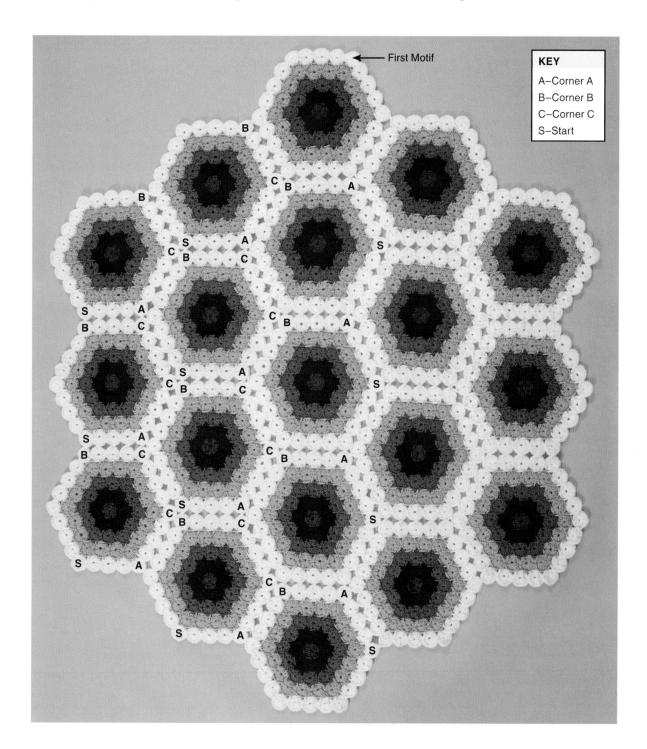

PILLOW
SKILL LEVEL

INTERMEDIATE

FINISHED SIZE
15¾ inches across

MATERIALS
- Red Heart Classic medium (worsted) weight yarn (3½ oz/ 190 yds/99g per skein):
  1 skein each #1 white, #615 artichoke, #759 cameo rose, #760 new berry and #339 mid brown

4
MEDIUM

- Size J/10/6mm crochet hook or size needed to obtain gauge
- 16-inch round pillow form

GAUGE
1 yo-yo = 1¾ inches in diameter

PATTERN NOTES
Stitches used in this pattern are found in the Stitch Guide unless otherwise stated in Special Stitches.

When joining, drop loop from hook, insert hook in place indicated and pull dropped loop through.

SPECIAL STITCHES
Small shell (sm shell): 3 dc in place indicated.

Medium shell (med shell): 9 dc in place indicated.

Large shell (lg shell): 12 dc in place indicated.

INSTRUCTIONS
PILLOW
FIRST MOTIF
Rnd 1: With mid brown, ch 3, 17 dc in 3rd ch from hook *(rem 2 chs of beg ch-3 counts as first dc)*, **join** *(see Pattern Notes)* in 3rd ch of beg ch-3. Fasten off.

Rnd 2: With new berry, ch 36, 2 dc in 3rd ch from hook *(first 2 chs count as first dc)*, join to any dc on rnd 1, 3 dc in same ch as last dc, *sk next 2 chs, sc in next ch**, sk next 2 chs, 2 dc in next ch, sk next 2 dc on rnd 1, join in next dc, **sm shell** *(see Special Stitches)* in same ch as last dc, rep from * around, ending last rep at **, join in 2nd ch of beg 2 chs. **Do not turn.**

Rnd 3: Lg shell *(see Special Stitches)* in ch at bottom of each sm shell around with sc between shells, join in beg dc of first large shell. Fasten off.

Rnd 4: With cameo rose, ch 72, 2 dc in 3rd ch from hook, join to 6th dc to left of any sc on last rnd, sm shell in same ch as last dc *(corner)*, work the following steps to complete rnd:

A. Sk next 2 chs, sc in next ch, sk next 2 chs;

B. 2 dc in next ch, sk next 2 dc on same yo-yo, join in next dc in same yo-yo as last joining, sm shell in same ch as last dc, join in 3rd dc on next yo-yo, 2 dc in same ch as last dc;

C. Rep step A;

D. 2 dc in next ch, sk next 2 dc on same yo-yo of last rnd, join in next dc, sm shell in same ch as last dc;

E. Rep steps A–D around, ending last rep with step B;

F. Sk next 2 chs, sc in last ch, join in 3rd ch of beg ch-3. **Do not turn.**

Rnd 5: Lg shell in same ch at bottom of next sm shell, sc in sp between shells, **med shell** *(see Special Stitches)* in ch at bottom of each sm shell around with sc between shells and lg shell in each corner, join in first dc of beg large shell. Fasten off.

Rnd 6: With artichoke, ch 108, 2 dc in 3rd ch from hook, join to 6th dc to left of any sc on last rnd at corner, sm shell in same ch as last dc *(corner)*, work the following steps to complete rnd:

A. Sk next 2 chs, sc in next ch, sk next 2 chs;

B. 2 dc in next ch, sk next 2 dc on same yo-yo, join in next dc in same yo-yo as last joining, sm shell in same ch as last dc, join in 3rd dc on next yo-yo, 2 dc in same ch as last dc;

C. Rep steps A, B and A;

D. 2 dc in next ch, sk next 2 dc on same yo-yo of last rnd, join in next dc, sm shell in same ch as last dc *(corner)*;

E. Rep steps A–D around, ending last rep with step B;

F. Sk next 2 chs, sc in last ch, join in 3rd ch of beg ch-3. **Do not turn.**

Rnd 7: Lg shell in same ch at bottom of next sm shell, sc in sp between shells, med shell in ch at bottom of each sm shell around with sc in sp between shells and lg shell in each corner, join in first dc of beg large shell. Fasten off.

Rnd 8: With white, ch 144, 2 dc in 3rd ch from hook, join to 6th dc to left of any sc on last rnd at corner, sm shell in same ch as last dc *(corner)*, work the following steps to complete rnd:

A. Sk next 2 chs, sc in next ch, sk next 2 chs;

B. 2 dc in next ch, sk next 2 dc on same yo-yo, join in next dc in same yo-yo as last joining, sm shell in same ch as last dc, join in 3rd dc on next yo-yo, 2 dc in same ch as last dc *(corner)*;

C. [Rep steps A and B] twice, rep step A;

D. 2 dc in next ch, sk next 2 dc on same yo-yo of last rnd, join in next dc, sm shell in same ch as last dc *(corner)*;

E. Rep steps A–D around;

F. Sk next ch, sc in last ch, join in 3rd ch of beg ch-3. **Do not turn.**

Rnd 9: Lg shell in same ch at bottom of next sm shell at corner, sc in sp between shells, med shell in ch at bottom of each sm shell around with sc between shells and lg shell in each corner, join in first dc of beg large shell. Fasten off.

2ND MOTIF
Rnds 1–8: Rep rnds 1–8 of First Motif.

Rnd 9: *(5 dc, join to 5th dc of corresponding yo-yo, 2 dc, sk next 2 dc on same corresponding yo-yo, join in next dc, 5 dc) in ch at bottom of next sm shell of yo-yo on First Motif, sc in sp between shells, [4 dc in ch at bottom of next sm shell, join in center dc of next yo-yo on First Motif, 4 dc in same ch as last dc, sc in sp between shells] 3 times, sc in sp between shells, rep from * around, inserting pillow form before closing, join in first dc. Fasten off. ■

Clover Patch

SKILL LEVEL

◼◼◼◻
INTERMEDIATE

FINISHED SIZES
Place Mat: 12¼ x 17½ inches
Hot Pad: 10½ inches square

MATERIALS
- Pisgah Yarn and Dyeing Co. Peaches & Creme medium (worsted) weight cotton yarn (2½ oz/122 yds/71g per ball): **4 MEDIUM**
  3 balls each #7 ivory and #56 celery
  1 ball #52 light sage
- Size I/9/5.5mm crochet hook or size needed to obtain gauge

GAUGE
1 yo-yo = 1¾ inches in diameter

PATTERN NOTES
Stitches used in this pattern are found in the Stitch Guide unless otherwise stated in Special Stitches.

When joining, drop loop from hook, insert hook in place indicated and pull dropped loop through.

SPECIAL STITCHES
Small shell (sm shell): 3 dc in place indicated.

Small joining shell (sm joining shell): 4 dc in place indicated.

Medium shell (med shell): 7 dc in place indicated.

Medium joining shell (med joining shell): 8 dc in place indicated.

Large shell (lg shell): 11 dc in place indicated

INSTRUCTIONS
PLACE MAT
**MAKE 2 WITH CELERY, LIGHT SAGE, IVORY, IVORY, CELERY AND IVORY.
MAKE 2 WITH IVORY, LIGHT SAGE, CELERY, CELERY, IVORY AND CELERY.**

Row 1: With celery or ivory, ch 42, **med shell** (*see Special Stitches*) in 3rd ch from hook, *sk next 2 chs**, sc in next ch, sk next 2 chs, med shell in next ch, rep from * across, ending last rep at **, sl st in next ch, **do not turn.**

Row 2: Working back across ch on row 1, *med shell in ch at bottom of next med shell**, sc in sp between shells, rep from * across, ending last rep at **, **join** (*see Pattern Notes*) in 2nd ch of beg ch on row 1. Fasten off.

Row 3: With light sage, ch 42, **sm joining shell** (*see Special Stitches*) in 3rd ch from hook, join in 4th dc of first yo-yo, **sm shell** (*see Special Stitches*) in same ch as last sm joining shell, *sk next 2 chs**, sc in next ch, sk next 2 chs, (sm joining shell, join in 4th dc of next yo-yo, sm shell) in next ch, rep from * across, ending last rep at **, sl st in last ch, **do not turn.**

Row 4: Working back across ch of last row, med shell in ch at bottom of next shell, [sc in sp between shells, med shell in ch at bottom of next med shell] across, join in 2nd ch of beg ch of last row. Fasten off.

Rnd 5: Now working in rnds, with ivory/celery, ch 84, sm shell in 3rd ch from hook, [sk next 2 chs, sc in next ch, sk next 2 chs, med shell in next ch] 5 times, [sk next 2 chs, sc in next ch, sk next 2 chs, sm shell in next ch] twice, [sk next 2 chs, sc in next ch, sk next 2 chs, (sm joining shell, join to 4th dc of last med shell worked, sm shell) in next ch] 5 times, sk next 2 chs, sc in next ch, sk next 2 chs, sm shell in next ch, sk next 2 chs, sl st in last ch, join to 2nd ch of beg ch-2.

Rnd 6: Working on opposite side of ch of rnd 5, **med joining shell** (see Special Stitches) in ch at bottom of last sm shell worked, join to center dc of first yo-yo on last row, sm shell in same ch, [sc in sp between shells, (sm joining shell, join to center dc of next med shell, sm shell) in ch at bottom of next shell] 5 times, sc in sp between shells, (sm joining shell, join to center dc of next yo-yo, med shell) in next ch at bottom of next shell, sc in sp between yo-yos, **lg shell** (see Special Stitches) in next ch at bottom of next sm shell, sc in sp between shells, [med shell in ch at bottom of next shell, sc in sp between shells] 5 times, lg shell in ch of next sm shell, sc in sp between yo-yos, join in beg dc of first med joining shell. Fasten off.

Rnds 7 & 8: Rep rnds 5 and 6.

Rnds 9 & 10: With celery/ivory, rep rnds 5 and 6.

Rnds 11 & 12: Rep rnds 5 and 6.

HOT PAD

Row 1: With celery, ch 36, **med shell** (see Special Stitches) in 3rd ch from hook, *sk next 2 chs**, sc in next ch, sk next 2 chs, med shell in next ch, rep from * across, ending last rep at **, sl st in next ch, **do not turn.**

Row 2: Working back across ch on row 1, *med shell in ch at bottom of next med shell**, sc in sp between shells, rep from * across, ending last rep at **, **join** (see Pattern Notes) in 2nd ch of beg ch on row 1. Fasten off.

Row 3: With ivory, ch 36, **sm joining shell** (see Special Stitches) in 3rd ch from hook, join in 4th dc of first yo-yo, sm shell in same ch as last sm joining shell, *sk next 2 chs**, sc in next ch,

sk next 2 chs, (sm joining shell, join in 4th dc of next yo-yo, **sm shell**—see Special Stitches) in next ch, rep from * across, ending last rep at **, sl st in last ch, **do not turn.**

Row 4: Working back across ch of last row, med shell in ch at bottom of next shell, [sc in sp between shells, med shell in ch at bottom of next med shell] across, join in 2nd ch of beg ch of last row. Fasten off.

Rnd 5: Now working in rnds, with light sage, ch 72, sm shell in 3rd ch from hook, [sk next 2 chs, sc in next ch, sk next 2 chs, med shell in next ch] 4 times, [sk next 2 chs, sc in next ch, sk next 2 chs, sm shell in next ch] twice, [sk next 2 chs, sc in next ch, sk next 2 chs, (sm joining shell, join to 4th dc of last med shell w͟o͟r͟k͟e͟d͟, s͟m͟ ͟s͟h͟e͟l͟l͟)͟ times, sk next 2 ͟c͟h͟s͟, s͟m shell in n͟ ͟c͟h, join to 2͟ ͟ ͟ ͟ ͟b͟e͟

Rnd 6: W͟o͟r͟k͟i͟n͟g͟ ͟o͟n͟ ͟o͟p͟p͟o͟s͟i͟t͟e͟ ͟s͟i͟d͟e͟ of ch of rnd 5, m͟e͟d͟ ͟j͟o͟i͟n͟i͟n͟g͟ ͟s͟h͟e͟l͟l͟ (see Special Stitches) in c͟h͟ ͟a͟t͟ ͟b͟o͟t͟t͟o͟m͟ ͟o͟f͟ last sm shell worked, join to ce͟n͟t͟e͟r͟ ͟d͟c͟ ͟o͟f͟ first yo-yo on last row, sm shell in sa͟m͟e͟ ͟c͟h͟, [sc in sp between shells, (sm joining sh͟e͟l͟l͟, join to center dc of next yo-yo, sm shell) in c͟h at bottom of next shell] times, sc in sp between shells, (sm joining shell, join to center dc of next yo-yo, med shell) in ch at bottom of next shell, sc in sp between shells, **lg shell** (see Special Stitches) in next shell, sc in sp between next shells, [med shell in ch at bottom of next shell, sc in sp between shells] 4 times, lg shell in ch of next sm shell, sc in sp between yo-yos, join in beg dc of first med joining shell. Fasten off.

Rnds 7 & 8: With celery, rep rnds 5 and 6. ■

STITCH GUIDE

STITCH ABBREVIATIONS

beg . . . . begin/begins/beginning
bpdc . . . . back post double crochet
bpsc . . . . .back post single crochet
bptr . . . . .back post treble crochet
CC. . . . . contrasting color
ch(s) . . . . .chain(s)
ch- . . . . .refers to chain or space
. . . . previously made (i.e., ch-1 space)
ch sp(s) . . . . chain space(s)
cl(s) . . . . cluster(s)
cm . . . . centimeter(s)
dc. . . . . double crochet (singular/plural)
dc dec . . . . double crochet 2 or more
. . . . stitches together, as indicated
dec. . . . . decrease/decreases/decreasing
dtr . . . . double treble crochet
ext . . . . .extended
fpdc. . . . . .front post double crochet
fpsc . . . . front post single crochet
fptr . . . . front post treble crochet
g . . . . .gram(s)
hdc . . . . half double crochet
hdc dec . . . . .half double crochet 2 or more
. . . . stitches together, as indicated
inc . . . . increase/increases/increasing
lp(s) . . . . .loop(s)
MC . . . . .main color
mm . . . . millimeter(s)
oz . . . . ounce(s)
pc . . . . popcorn(s)
rem .remain/remains/remaining
rep(s) . . . . .repeat(s)
rnd(s) . . . . round(s)
RS . . . . right side
sc . . . . single crochet (singular/plural)
sc dec . . . . .single crochet 2 or more
. . . . stitches together, as indicated
sk . . . . .skip/skipped/skipping
sl st(s). . . . . slip stitch(es)
sp(s) . . . . space(s)/spaced
st(s) . . . . .stitch(es)
tog. . . . . .together
tr. . . . . treble crochet
trtr. . . . . .triple treble
WS . . . . wrong side
yd(s) . . . . .yard(s)
yo. . . . . yarn over

YARN CONVERSION

OUNCES TO GRAMS		GRAMS TO OUNCES	
1	28.4	25	⅞
2	56.7	40	1⅔
3	85.0	50	1¾
4	113.4	100	3½

UNITED STATES		UNITED KINGDOM
sl st (slip stitch)	=	sc (single crochet)
sc (single crochet)	=	dc (double crochet)
hdc (half double crochet)	=	htr (half treble crochet)
dc (double crochet)	=	tr (treble crochet)
tr (treble crochet)	=	dtr (double treble crochet)
dtr (double treble crochet)	=	ttr (triple treble crochet)
skip	=	miss

Single crochet decrease (sc dec):
(Insert hook, yo, draw lp through) in each of the sts indicated, yo, draw through all lps on hook.

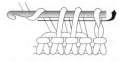

Example of 2-sc dec

Half double crochet decrease (hdc dec):
(Yo, insert hook, yo, draw lp through) in each of the sts indicated, yo, draw through all lps on hook.

Example of 2-hdc dec

Reverse Single Crochet (reverse sc):
Ch 1. Skip first st. [Working from left to right, insert hook in next st from front to back, draw up lp on hook, yo, and draw through both lps on hook.]

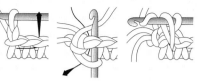

Chain (ch):
Yo, pull through lp on hook.

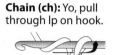

Single crochet (sc):
Insert hook in st, yo, pull through st, yo, pull through both lps on hook.

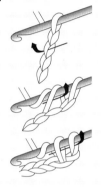

Double crochet (dc):
Yo, insert hook in st, yo, pull through st, [yo, pull through 2 lps] twice.

Double crochet decrease (dc dec):
Yo, insert hook, yo, draw loop through, draw through 2 lps on hook) in each of the sts indicated, yo, draw through all lps on hook.

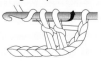

Example of 2-dc dec

Front loop (front lp) Back loop (back lp)
Front Loop   Back Loop

Front post stitch (fp): Back post stitch (bp):
When working post st, insert hook from right to left around post st on previous row.

Back   Front

Post of Stitch

Half double crochet (hdc):
Yo, insert hook in st, yo, pull through st, yo, pull through all 3 lps on hook.

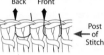

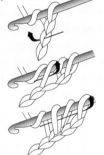

Double treble crochet (dtr):
Yo 3 times, insert hook in st, yo, pull through st, [yo, pull through 2 lps] 4 times.

Treble crochet decrease (tr dec):
Holding back last lp of each st, tr in each of the sts indicated, yo, pull through all lps on hook.

Example of 2-tr dec

Slip stitch (sl st):
Insert hook in st, pull through both lps on hook.

Chain Color Change (ch color change)
Yo with new color, draw through last lp on hook.

Double Crochet Color Change (dc color change)
Drop first color, yo with new color, draw through last 2 lps of st.

Treble crochet (tr):
Yo twice, insert hook in st, yo, pull through st, [yo, pull through 2 lps] 3 times.

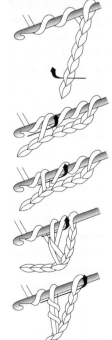

Metric Conversion Charts

METRIC CONVERSIONS

yards	x	.9144	=	metres (m)
yards	x	91.44	=	centimetres (cm)
inches	x	2.54	=	centimetres (cm)
inches	x	25.40	=	millimetres (mm)
inches	x	.0254	=	metres (m)

centimetres	x	.3937	=	inches
metres	x	1.0936	=	yards

INCHES INTO MILLIMETRES & CENTIMETRES (Rounded off slightly)

inches	mm	cm	inches	cm	inches	cm	inches	cm
1/8	3	0.3	5	12.5	21	53.5	38	96.5
1/4	6	0.6	5 1/2	14	22	56	39	99
3/8	10	1	6	15	23	58.5	40	101.5
1/2	13	1.3	7	18	24	61	41	104
5/8	15	1.5	8	20.5	25	63.5	42	106.5
3/4	20	2	9	23	26	66	43	109
7/8	22	2.2	10	25.5	27	68.5	44	112
1	25	2.5	11	28	28	71	45	114.5
1 1/4	32	3.2	12	30.5	29	73.5	46	117
1 1/2	38	3.8	13	33	30	76	47	119.5
1 3/4	45	4.5	14	35.5	31	79	48	122
2	50	5	15	38	32	81.5	49	124.5
2 1/2	65	6.5	16	40.5	33	84	50	127
3	75	7.5	17	43	34	86.5		
3 1/2	90	9	18	46	35	89		
4	100	10	19	48.5	36	91.5		
4 1/2	115	11.5	20	51	37	94		

KNITTING NEEDLES CONVERSION CHART

Canada/U.S.	0	1	2	3	4	5	6	7	8	9	10	10½	11	13	15
Metric (mm)	2	2¼	2¾	3¼	3½	3¾	4	4½	5	5½	6	6½	8	9	10

CROCHET HOOKS CONVERSION CHART

Canada/U.S.	1/B	2/C	3/D	4/E	5/F	6/G	8/H	9/I	10/J	10½/K	N
Metric (mm)	2.25	2.75	3.25	3.5	3.75	4.25	5	5.5	6	6.5	9.0

Annie's Attic®

TOLL-FREE ORDER LINE (800) LV-ANNIE (800) 582-6643
Customer Service (800) AT-ANNIE (800) 282-6643, **Fax** (800) 882-6643
Visit AnniesAttic.com
We have made every effort to ensure the accuracy and completeness of these instructions.
We cannot, however, be responsible for human error, typographical mistakes or variations in individual work.

ISBN: 978-1-59635-314-5